For

Sisters

Compiled by
Claudine Gandolfi
Illustrated by Katharine Barnwell

PETER PAUPER PRESS, INC.
WHITE PLAINS, NEW YORK

To Michele,
my sister, my shadow, my friend

Copyright © 1997
Peter Pauper Press, Inc.
202 Mamaroneck Avenue
White Plains, NY 10601
ISBN 0-88088-815-6
Printed in China
7 6 5 4 3 2 1

Sisters

Introduction

*W*hat can be said of the bond that sisters share? It can be a closeness beyond compare or, at times, a little too close for comfort. Our shared rooms, "borrowed" clothes, mutual secrets, disagreements, and fights are par for the course. As sisters, we know that no matter what happens between us, we will always have each other.

C. G.

A sister can be your
conscience, your confidante,
and your champion.

*N*o one can understand
you like your sister. She's
comprised of all the same
parts you are.

To most people, my sister and I didn't seem to have much in common; but I knew . . . that we were remarkably alike.

KATHLEEN NORRIS

*A*dvances towards heroism
in her sister made Elinor feel
equal to anything herself.

JANE AUSTEN,
Sense and Sensibility

There is something so physical about sisterhood; some body-memory, too deep for words.

KENNEDY FRASER

*K*risten and Katy are my youngest sisters. Although we have different fathers, I don't think of them as half-sisters at all. They are complete sisters in all senses of the word, unstinting in their teasing and devotion. . . . And if they were not my sisters, I'd want to be their friend.

BRETT BUTLER

I secretly began to keep score and I quickly realized that I was right. Mom did think my sister was more beautiful than I was. On the other hand, I was much more sociable and charming. People liked me more than Leigh, who was a real brat. I could live with that.

CANDY,
quoted in Mom Loved You Best

We had problems for a long time because we both thought we were Mom's favorite child. We talked over our feelings about this four years ago and realized it didn't matter who was the favorite. Now we're just happy we have each other.

ANONYMOUS,
quoted by Francine Klagsbrun in
Mixed Feelings

*T*he sister bond is often
greater than that with a friend
or a brother . . .

DR. HARRIETTE MCADOO

I'm three and you're four.
PRINCESS ELIZABETH,
speaking of their places in line for
the throne of England

No, you're not. *I'm* three,
you're *seven*.

PRINCESS MARGARET,
speaking of their ages

No matter how often you quarrel, a sister will always forgive you in the end.

[*My* sisters and I] have dinner-table debates about whether it's better to establish a career first or plan a family first. But the discussions are really just for fun, since we're all so different we couldn't have imitated each other if we'd tried.

KATHY SPARKMAN

[*M*y sister] accommodates me, never reproaches me with her doctrine, never tries to change me. She accepts and loves me, despite our differences.

JOY HARJO

I used to get on Phylicia's
nerves when I was a little girl.
                              DEBBIE ALLEN

It was worse than that.
Whenever she came around
me, I got into trouble.
                              PHYLICIA RASHAD

*T*here is a space within sisterhood for likeness and difference, for the subtle differences that challenge and delight; there is space for disappointment—and surprise.

CHRISTINE DOWNING

$\mathcal{I}$t's just hard because [being sisters] you hold in a lot of stuff. You don't want to outshine; you don't want to upstage, and then you don't want to get too far back in the background, either.

JUNE POINTER

Your siblings are the only
people in the world who
know what it's like to have
been brought up the way
you were.

BETSY COHEN

We delighted in being competent—more competent than the one in the family who was spacy, the one who was overemotional. We just had things together, and we understood the world.

DEBRA SPARK

*L*iving with a sister is easier
than moving in with a friend.
When your new roommate
is not a family member, you
both act like nervous
newlyweds.

JEANIE PYUN

I suppose there are sisters
who don't compete. I have
never met one.

LISA GRUNWALD

A sister can be seen as someone who is both ourselves and very much not ourselves—a special kind of double.

TONI A. H. McNARON

"My dear Jane!" exclaimed Elizabeth, "you are too good. Your sweetness and disinterestedness are really angelic; I do not know what to say to you. I feel as if I had never done you justice, or loved you as you deserve."

JANE AUSTEN,
Pride and Prejudice

*S*he looks up to me and tries to copy everything that I do, which is partly really adorable and partly kind of annoying. Sometimes I get to a point where I just want to say "Okay, please leave me alone for a while now." But Christina still follows me around.

DOMINIQUE MOCEANU

*F*or there is no friend like a sister
In calm or stormy weather;
To cheer one on the tedious way,
To fetch one if one goes astray,
To lift one if one totters down,
To strengthen whilst one stands.

CHRISTINA ROSSETTI,
Goblin Market

It is true that I was born in Iowa, but I can't speak for my twin sister.

ABIGAIL VAN BUREN

*O*ne of the best things
about being an adult is the
realization that you can share
with your sister and still have
plenty for yourself.

BETSY COHEN

I think if there's no sibling rivalry in a family, there's a lot of denial going on, because you can't help but rub against each other when you're forming who you are.

JOANNA KERNS

*C*hildren of the same
mother do not always agree.
NIGERIAN PROVERB

I cannot deny that, now
I am without your company I
feel not only that I am
deprived of a very dear sister,
but that I have lost half of
myself.

BEATRICE D'ESTE,
from a letter to her sister Isabella

*A*s young children, my sisters and I were close. I enjoyed being the oldest, showing them around, protecting them. When a bully who sat across from Susan at the schoolroom table kicked her legs black-and-blue, I beat him up in the playground.

PATRICIA IRELAND

*A*ll three sisters had the same high-bridged noses . . . I pored over these pictures, intrigued by the idea of the triplicate, identical noses. I did not have a sister myself, then, and the mystique of sisterhood was potent for me.

MARGARET ATWOOD

*A*shley is the part of my mom that [my mom] likes best. She's intellectual, organized, such a hostess.

WYNONNA JUDD

If you and your sister take time to do things one-on-one, away from the extended family, a new pattern of dealing with each other—and a new friendship—is free to emerge.

KIM WRIGHT WILEY

$\mathcal{S}$isters—they share the agony and the exhilaration. As youngsters they may share popsicles, chewing gum, hair dryers and bedrooms. When they grow up, they share confidences, careers and children, and some even chat for hours every day.

ROXANNE BROWN

My oldest sister, Alice Lynn Foran . . . is the rock, the one you can call at three in the morning, and she'll always be ready to help in any way.

REBA MCENTIRE

I'll miss not having any-
body on the same page as me.
When I want to pass, [Tauja]
is always in the place where I
pass.

TAMIKA CATCHINGS,
basketball player, age 16,
at Stevenson High School
whose sister is graduating

*C*an you imagine what it's
like to wish more than
anything in the world to be
like your sister and know
that you can't?

NANCY,
quoted by
Francine Klagsbrun in
Mixed Feelings

*M*ama came from a family
of many sisters. And she
preached to us endlessly
about the necessity of living
in harmony with one another.

BELL HOOKS

*M*y sister had a game . . .
called "The Elder Sister." The
theme was that in our family
was an elder sister, senior to
my sister and myself. She was
mad and lived in a cave at
Corbin's Head, but sometimes
she came to the house. . . .
Why did I *like* being terrified?

AGATHA CHRISTIE

$\mathcal{M}$om sent me to the pantry for flour and I put a half-eaten Milky Way bar on the counter. When I came back, Sheila was eating it. Sheila is the one person on earth who can easily reduce me to the emotions and mentality of a six-year-old.

DEBORAH PERRY

[*I*] asked for her advice and help. It was a homecoming of sorts. I can still recall the fullness in her voice when she told me how very, very touched she was that at last I was letting her in.

MARCIA ANN GILLESPIE,
about her sister Charlene

*I*t's hard as kids to know what's causing you to feel and react the way you do, but as adults, we worked through a lot of that stuff. Now we're each other's best supporters. No one knows her better than I know her, and vice versa.

JOANNA KERNS

Only a sister can compare
the sleek body that now exists
with the chubby body hidden
underneath. Only a sister
knows about former pimples,
failing math, and underwear
kicked under the bed.

LAURA TRACY

*I*f your sister is in a tearing
hurry to go out and cannot
catch your eye, she's wearing
your best sweater.

PAM BROWN

*E*ven when [my sister and I]
are separated by continents,
we are moving through time
in parallel tracks.

KENNEDY FRASER

A ministering angel shall
my sister be.

SHAKESPEARE,
Hamlet

*M*y sister! my sweet sister!
  if a name
Dearer and purer were, it
should be thine.

BYRON,
Epistle to Augusta

I wish dolphin were by my side, in a bath, bright blue, with her tail curled. But then I've always been in love with her since I was a green eyed brat under the nursery table, and so shall remain in my extreme senility.

VIRGINIA WOOLF,
about her sister, Vanessa Bell

*B*essie and I have been
together since time began, or
so it seems. Bessie is my little
sister, only she's not so little.
She is 101 years old, and I'm
103. . . . After so long, we are
in some ways like one person.

SARAH L. "SADIE" DELANY

I wrote a long letter to Santa Claus and said that I had been particularly good that year and felt I was quite deserving. I ended with, "I look forward to seeing you." Then I added, "P.S. My turtle died two days ago. I hope my sister's turtle dies too."

FRANCINE KLAGSBRUN,
Mixed Feelings

*S*he never judges me, and through the many [rehab] treatments she's always been supportive. Not in a caretaking way, but she's always wanted me to be all right.

CARRIE MORROW,
about her sister,
Jennifer Jason Leigh

We'd fall asleep holding
onto each other's hair.

ASHLEY JUDD,
About her sister Wynonna

*L*istening to my sister sing
has been one of the greatest
gifts of my life.

NORMAN BUCKLEY,
brother of Betty Buckley

$\mathcal{S}$isterhood is to friendship what an arranged marriage is to romance. You are thrown together for life, no questions asked (until later), no chance of escape. And if you're lucky, you find love despite the confinement.

LISA GRUNWALD

One of the nicest things about those early years on the bus was being together with Louise and Irlene, just as we had been as children. . . . I was still able to play Big Sister to the hilt, coaching my sisters about their roles in the band but also relying on them for help with Matthew.

BARBARA MANDRELL

[Emily's] love was poured out on Anne, as Charlotte's was on her. But the affection among all the three was stronger than either death or life.

ELIZABETH GASKELL,
on the Brontë Sisters

*N*ever praise a sister to a sister, in the hope of your compliments reaching the proper ears.

RUDYARD KIPLING

I grew up with a sister four years older than I who's very pretty, the quintessential California girl. I had been this beanpole, and I didn't think that I was anything special.

MOLLY RINGWALD

I was the oldest girl. So, I was helping to raise my brothers and sisters and changing diapers and making lunches and breaking up fights. I speculate that's why I'm comfortable being the bandleader.

JOAN OSBORNE

*W*hatever you do they will love you; even if they don't love you they are connected to you till you die. You can be boring and tedious with sisters, whereas you have to put on a good face with friends.

DEBORAH MOGGACH

*M*y sisters are guaranteed friends for life. . . . There's never a reason to hurt your sisters. Never was, never will be.

KELLY TURLINGTON

I knew that my sister always loved me, that she'd always take care of me. But Alline was somehow too slow and quiet for me—I was always up to something, running, moving, doing.

TINA TURNER

*T*he difference between us is I will shop for something expensive but just buy one thing . . . Whereas Alex will buy 150 shirts and 150 cardigans . . . But they sit there and just accumulate and accumulate.

MARIE-CHANTAL MILLER,
on her sister Alexandra

$\mathcal{T}$o have a loving relationship with a sister is not simply to have a buddy or confidante—it is to have a soul mate for life.

VICTORIA SECUNDA

I'm the watcher. I like to observe, and [Joan] very much likes to participate. She likes to be center stage, and I like to sit in the background.

JACKIE COLLINS

*S*isters share secrets they can never tell mother.